Xavier de Maistre, Henry Attwell

A Journey Round my Room

Xavier de Maistre, Henry Attwell

A Journey Round my Room

ISBN/EAN: 9783744795241

Printed in Europe, USA, Canada, Australia, Japan

Cover: Foto ©Thomas Meinert / pixelio.de

More available books at **www.hansebooks.com**

A

Journey Round My Room

BY

XAVIER DE MAISTRE

TRANSLATED FROM THE FRENCH, WITH A
NOTICE OF THE AUTHOR'S LIFE

BY

H. A.

NEW YORK
PUBLISHED BY HURD AND HOUGHTON
Cambridge: Riverside Press
1871

PREFACE.

———◆———

THE author of the "Voyage autour de ma Chambre" was the younger brother of Count Joseph de Maistre, a well-known writer upon political and philosophical subjects. Chambéry was the place of their birth, but their family was of French origin. Both brothers were officers in the Sardinian army; and when Savoy was conquered by the French, Xavier de Maistre sought an asylum in Saint Petersburg, where his brother resided in the capacity of envoy from the court of Sardinia. Xavier entered the Russian army, distinguished himself in the war against Persia, and attained the rank of major-general.

Our interest in the "Voyage" is heightened by our knowledge that it was actually written during De Maistre's forty-two days' arrest at Turin, referred to in the third chapter. He sent the manuscript, which he regarded as a mere playful effort of his imagination, for his brother's perusal. Joseph was pleased with the book; and Xavier, who had an almost filial affection for his brother, was soon afterwards agreeably surprised by receiving, in place of his manuscript, the "Voyage" in print.

This success encouraged him to begin a sequel to the "Voyage." Joseph, however, disapproved of this new attempt. The "Expédition Nocturne" was, notwithstanding, finished, and was published some years later.

Xavier de Maistre's next production (1811) was "Le Lépreux de la Cité d'Aoste," a very touching and gracefully written narrative. It occupies but a few pages ; and, as it is to be found in almost every good anthology of French literature, is perhaps the best known of our author's works.

His other books are "Les Prisonniers du Caucase" (1815) and "La Jeune Sibérienne," both of them charming works, containing faithful pictures of domestic scenes with which we are little familiar through other sources.

From his childhood Xavier de Maistre was devoted to painting. He deservedly gained considerable reputation as a painter of miniature portraits and landscapes.

Nor did he neglect science while devoting himself to art and literature. He applied himself so successfully to the study of chemistry that he was able to communicate several valuable " Mémoires " to the Academy of Turin, of which he was a member.

Xavier de Maistre died (1852) at an advanced age in his adopted country, where he had married, and which he only quitted once, for a brief season.

———◆———

Some apology for publishing this translation is perhaps necessary.

Although in France the " Voyage " retains the high esteem in which it has been held for half a century, it is hardly known in England, except by those who are familiar with the French language and literature.

During the last twenty years the proportion of educated persons in this country who are unable to enjoy a French book in the original has greatly decreased. Still, there are some to whom a translation of this delightful work may be acceptable.

To them I offer the pleasant labor of a few leisure hours ; but not without assuring them that in endeavoring to reproduce faithfully the author's ideas, I have felt at every paragraph how true it is that "*le style se traduit pas,*" — "style is untranslatable.

———

The *headings* of the chapters are not De Maistre's. They appear in Tardieu's pretty little edition of the "Voyage." The miniatures, by M. Veyssier, are from the same source.

H. A.

CONTENTS.

———◆———

b

x   *Contents.*

Contents.   xi

I.

A Book of Discoveries.

WHAT more glorious than to open for one's self a new career, — to appear suddenly before the learned world with a book of discoveries in one's hand, like an unlooked-for comet blazing in the empyrean!

No longer will I keep my book in obscurity. Behold it, gentlemen; read it! I have undertaken and performed a forty-two days' journey round my room. The interesting observations I have made, and the constant pleasure I have experienced all along the road, made me wish to publish my travels; the certainty of being useful decided the matter. And when I think of the number of unhappy ones to whom I offer a never failing resource for weary moments, and a balm for the ills they suffer, my heart is filled with inexpressible satisfaction. The pleasure to be found in travelling round one's room is sheltered from the restless jealousy of men, and is independent of Fortune.

Surely there is no being so miserable as to be without a retreat to which he can withdraw and hide himself from the world. Such a hiding-place will contain all the preparations our journey requires.

Every man of sense will, I am sure, adopt my system, whatever may be his peculiar character or temperament. Be he miserly or prodigal, rich or poor, young or old, born beneath the torrid zone or near the poles, he may travel with me. Among the immense family of men who throng the earth, there is not one, no, not one (I mean of those who inhabit rooms), who, after reading this book can refuse his approbation of the new mode of travelling I introduce into the world.

Eulogy of the Journey.

I MIGHT fairly begin the eulogium of my journey by saying it has cost me nothing. This point merits attention. It will gain for it the praise and welcome of people of moderate means. And not of these only : there is another class with whom its success will, on this account, be even more certain. "And who are they?" you ask. Why, the rich, to be sure. And then, again, what a comfort the new mode of travelling will be to the sick ; they need not fear bleak winds or change of weather. And what a thing, too, it will be for cowards ; they will be safe from pitfalls or quagmires. Thousands who hitherto did not dare, others who were not able, and others to whom it never occurred to think of such a thing as going on a journey, will make up their minds to follow my example. Surely, the idlest person will not hesitate to set out with me on a pleasure jaunt which will cost him neither trouble nor money. Come then, let us start! Follow me, all ye whom the "pangs of despised love" or the slights of friends keep within doors, — follow me far from the meannesses and unkindnesses of men. Be ye unhappy, sick, or weary, follow me. Ye idle ones, arouse ye, one and all. And ye who brood over gloomy projects of reform and retreat, on account of some infidelity, — amiable anchorites of an evening's duration, who renounce the world for your boudoir, — come, and be led by me to banish these dark thoughts; you lose a moment's pleasure without gaining a moment's wisdom! Deign to accompany me on my journey. We will jog cheerfully and by easy stages

along the road of travellers who have seen
both Rome and Paris. No obstacle shall
hinder our way; and giving ourselves up
gaily to Imagination, we will follow her
whithersoever it may be her good pleasure
to lead us.

III.

Laws and Customs.

HOW many inquisitive people there are in the world! I am sure my reader wants to know why the journey round my room has lasted forty-two days rather than forty-three, or any other number. But how am I to tell him what I do not know myself? All I can say is, that if the work is too long for him, it is not my fault that it was not shorter. I dismiss all the pride a traveller may fairly indulge in, and candidly declare I should have been well contented, for my part, with a single chapter. It is quite true that I made myself as comfortable as possible in my room; but still, alas, I was not my own master in the matter of leaving it. Nay,

more, I even think that had it not been for
the intervention of certain powerful persons
who interested themselves in me, and towards whom I entertain a lively sense of
gratitude, I should have had ample time for
producing a folio volume ; so prejudiced in
my favor were the guardians who made me
travel round my room.

And yet, intelligent reader, see how
wrong these men were ; and understand
clearly, if you can, the argument I am
about to put before you.

Can there be anything more natural or
more just than to draw your sword upon a
man who happens to tread on your toe, who
lets slip a bitter word during a moment's
vexation caused by your own thoughtless-
ness, or who has had the misfortune to gain
favor in the sight of your lady-love ?

Under such or like circumstances, you
betake yourself to a meadow, and there, like
Nicole and the " Bourgeois Gentilhomme,"

you try to give the fourth cut while your
adversary parries tierce ; and, that ven-
geance may be fully satisfied, you present
your naked breast to him, thus running the
risk of being killed by your enemy, in order
to be avenged.

It is evident that such a custom is most
reasonable. And yet, we sometimes meet
with people who disapprove of so praise-
worthy a course. But what is about of a
piece with the rest of the business is, that
the very persons who condemn the course
we have described, and who would have
it regarded as a grave error, would judge
still more harshly any one who refused to
commit it. More than one unlucky wight
has, by endeavoring to conform to their
opinion, lost his reputation and his livelihood. So that, when people are so unfortunate as to have an affair of honor to settle, it would not be a bad plan to cast lots
to see whether it shall be arranged accord-

ing to law, or according to fashion.   And as law and fashion are at variance, the judges might decide upon their sentence by the aid of dice, — and probably it is to some such decision as this that we should have to refer in order to explain how it came about that my journey lasted just two and forty days.

IV.

Latitude and Topography.

MY room is situated in latitude 48°
. east, according to the measurement
of Father Beccaria. It lies east and west,
and, if you keep very close to the wall,
forms a parallelogram of thirty-six steps
round. My journey will, however, be
longer than this ; for I shall traverse my
room up and down and across, without rule
or plan. I shall even zig-zag about, following, if needs be, every possible geometrical
line. I am no admirer of people who are
such masters of their every step and every
idea that they can say : " To-morrow I shall
make three calls, write four letters, and
finish this or that work." So open is my
soul to all sorts of ideas, tastes, and feel-

ings ; so greedily does it absorb whatever
comes first, that . . . . but why should
it deny itself the delights that are scattered
along life's hard path ? So few and far between are they, that it would indeed be
senseless not to stop, and even turn aside,
to gather such as are placed within our
reach. Of these joys, none, to my thinking, is more attractive than following the
course of one's fancies as a hunter follows
his game, without pretending to keep to
any set route. Hence, when I travel in
my room, I seldom keep to a straight line.
From my table I go towards a picture
which is placed in a corner ; thence I set
out in an oblique direction for the door ;
and then, although on starting I had intended to return to my table, yet, if I
chance to fall in with my arm-chair on the
way, I at once, and most unceremoniously,
take up my quarters therein. By the by,
what a capital article of furniture an arm-

chair is, and, above all, how convenient to a thoughtful man. In long winter evenings it is ofttimes sweet, and always prudent, to stretch yourself therein, far from the bustle of crowded assemblies. A good fire, some books and pens ; what safeguards these against *ennui !* And how pleasant, again, to forget books and pens in order to stir the fire, while giving one's self up to some agreeable meditation, or stringing together a few rhymes for the amusement of friends, as the hours glide by and fall into eternity, without making their sad passage felt.

V.

The Bed.

NEXT to my arm-chair, as we go
northward, my bed comes into sight.
It is placed at the end of my room, and
forms the most agreeable perspective. It
is very pleasantly situated, and the earliest
rays of the sun play upon my curtains.
On fine summer days I see them come
creeping, as the sun rises, all along the
whitened wall. The elm-trees opposite my
windows divide them into a thousand pat-
terns as they dance upon my bed, and,
reflecting its rose-and-white color, shed a
charming tint around. I hear the confused twitter of the swallows that have
taken possession of my roof, and the war-
bling of the birds that people the elms.

Then do a thousand smiling fancies fill my soul; and in the whole universe no being enjoys an awakening so delightful, so peaceful, as mine.

I confess that I do indeed revel in these sweet moments, and prolong as far as I can the pleasure it gives me to meditate in the comfortable warmth of my bed. What scene can adapt itself so well to the imagination, and awaken such delicious ideas, as the couch on which my fancy floats me into the forgetfulness of self! Here it is that the mother, intoxicated with joy at the birth of a son, forgets her pangs. Hither it is that fantastic pleasures, the fruit of fancy or of hope, come to agitate us. In a word, it is here that during one half of a life-time we forget the annoyances of the other half.

But what a host of thoughts, some agreeable, some sad, throng my brain at once, — strange minglings of terrible and delicious pictures!

A bed sees us born, and sees us die. It is the ever changing scene upon which the human race play by turns interesting dramas, laughable farces, and fearful tragedies. It is a cradle decked with flowers. A throne of love. A sepulchre.

VI.

For Metaphysicians.

THIS chapter is for metaphysicians, and for metaphysicians only. It will throw. a great light upon man's nature. It is the prism with which to analyze and decompose the human faculties, by separating the animal force from the pure rays of intellect.

It would be impossible for me to explain how I came to burn my fingers at the very onset of my journey without expounding to my reader my system of the *Soul and the Animal.*[1] And besides, this metaphysical discovery has so great an influ-

[1] *Bête* is not translatable here. The English word *animal* is hardly nearer than *beast*. *Bête* is a milder word than *beast*, and when used metaphorically, implies silliness rather than brutality. In some cases our *creature* would translate it, *Pauvre bête ! Poor creature !*

ence on my thoughts and actions, that it would be very difficult to understand this book if I did not begin by giving the key to its meaning.

Various observations have enabled me to perceive that man is made up of a soul and an animal. These two beings are quite distinct, but they are so dovetailed one into the other, or upon the other, that the soul must, if we would make the distinction between them, possess a certain superiority over the animal.

I have it from an old professor (and this is as long ago as I can remember), that Plato used to call matter the OTHER. This is all very well; but I prefer giving this name *par excellence* to the animal which is joined to our soul. This substance it is which is really the OTHER, and which plays such strange tricks upon us. It is easy enough to see, in a sort of general way, that man is twofold. But this, they say, is because he is made up of soul and body ; and they accuse the body of I don't know how many things, and very inconsistently, seeing that it can neither feel nor think. It is upon the animal that the blame should fall ; upon that sensitive being, which, while it is perfectly distinct from the soul, is a real individual, enjoying a separate existence, with its own tastes, inclinations, and will, and which only ranks higher than other animals, because it is better educated than they, and is provided with more perfect organs.

Ladies and gentlemen ! Be as proud of your intellect as you please, but be very suspicious of the OTHER, especially when you are together.

I have experimented I know not how oft, upon the union of these two heterogeneous creatures. I have, for instance, clearly ascertained that the soul can make herself obeyed by the animal, and that, by way of retaliation, the animal makes the soul act contrary to its own inclination. The one, as a rule, has the legislative, the other the executive power, but these two are often at variance. The great business of a man of genius is to train his animal well, in order that it may go alone, while the soul, delivered from this troublesome companion, can raise herself to the skies.

But this requires illustration. When, sir, you are reading a book, and an agreeable idea suddenly enters your imagination, your soul attaches herself to the new idea at once, and forgets the book, while your eyes follow mechanically the words and lines. You get through the page without understanding it, and without remembering what you have read. Now this is because your soul, having ordered her companion to read to her, gave no warning of the short absence she contemplated, so that the OTHER went on reading what the soul no longer attended to.

VII.

The Soul.

IS not this clear to you? Let us illus-
trate it still farther.

One day last summer at an appointed
hour, I was wending my way to court. I
had been sketching all day, and my soul,
choosing to meditate upon painting, left
the duty of taking me to the king's palace
to the animal.

How sublime, thought my soul, is the
painter's art! Happy is he who is touched
by the aspect of nature, and does not
depend upon his pictures for a livelihood ;
who does not paint solely as a pastime, but
struck with the majesty of a beautiful form,
and the wonderful way in which the light
with its thousand tints plays upon the

human face, strives to imitate in his works the wonderful effects of nature! Happy, too, is the painter who is led by love of landscape into solitary paths, and who can make his canvas breathe the feeling of sadness with which he is inspired by a gloomy wood or a desert plain. His productions imitate and reproduce nature. He creates new seas and dark caverns into which the sun has never peered. At his command, coppices of evergreens spring into life, and the blue of heaven is reflected on his pictures. He darkens the air, and we hear the roar of the storm. At another time he presents to the eye of the wondering beholder the delightful plains of ancient Sicily: startled nymphs flee the pursuit of a satyr through the bending reeds; temples of stately architecture raise their grand fronts above the sacred forest that surrounds them. Imagination loses itself among the still paths of this ideal country.

Bluish backgrounds blend with the sky, and the whole landscape, reproduced in the waters of a tranquil river, forms a scene that no tongue can describe.

While my soul was thus reflecting, the *other* went its way, Heaven knows whither! Instead of going to court, according to orders, it took such a turn to the left, that my soul just caught it up at Madame de Hautcastel's door, full half a mile from the Palais Royal!

Now I leave the reader to fancy what might have been the consequence had the truant visited so beautiful a lady alone.

VIII.

The Animal.

IF it is both useful and agreeable to have a soul so disengaged from matter that we can let it travel alone whenever we please, this has also its disadvantages. Through this, for instance, I got the burn I spoke of a few chapters back.

I generally leave my animal to prepare my breakfast. Its care it is to slice and toast my bread. My coffee it makes admirably, and helps itself thereto without my soul's concerning herself in the transaction. But this is a very rare and nice performance to execute ; for though it is easy enough while busied in a mechanical operation, to think of something quite different, it is extremely difficult, so to speak, to watch one's self-work, or, if I express myself systematically, to employ one's soul to examine the animal's progress, and to watch its work without taking part in it. This is the most extraordinary metaphysical feat a man can execute.

I had rested my tongs on the embers to toast my bread, and some little time afterwards, while my soul was travelling, a burning stick fell on the hearth : my poor animal seized the tongs, and I burnt my fingers.

IX.

Philosophy.

I HOPE I have sufficiently developed my ideas in the foregoing chapters to furnish you, good reader, with matter for thought, and to enable you to make discoveries along the brilliant career before you. You cannot be other than highly satisfied with yourself if you succeed in the long run in making your soul travel alone. The pleasure afforded by this power will amply counterbalance any inconvenience that may arise from it. What more flattering delight is there than the being able thus to expand one's existence, to occupy at once earth and heaven, to double, so to speak, one's being? Is it not man's eternal, insatiable desire to augment his strength and his faculties, to be where he is not, to recall the past, and live in the future? He would fain command armies, preside over learned societies, and be the idol of the fair. And, if he attain to all this, then he regrets the tranquillity of a rural life, and envies the shepherd's cot. His plans, his hopes, are constantly foiled by the ills that flesh is heir to. He can find happiness nowhere. A quarter of an hour's journey with me will show him the way to it.

Ah, why does he not leave to the OTHER those carking cares and that tormenting ambition. Come, my poor friend! Make but an effort to burst from thy prison, and from the height of heaven, whither I am about to lead thee, from the midst of the celestial shades, from the empyrean itself, behold thy *animal* run along the road to fortune and honor. See with what gravity it walks among men. The crowd falls back with respect, and believe me, none will remark that it is alone. The people among whom it walks care very little whether it has a soul or not, whether it thinks or not. A thousand sentimental women will fall desperately in love with it without discovering the defect. It may even raise itself without thy soul's help to the highest favor and fortune. Nay, I should not be astonished if, on thy return from the empyrean, thy soul, on getting home, were to find itself in the *animal* of a noble lord.

X.

The Portrait.

BUT you must not let yourself think that instead of keeping my promise to describe my journey round my room, I am beating the bush to see how I can evade the difficulty. This would be a great mistake on your part. For our journey is really going on ; and while my soul, falling back on her own resources, was in the last chapter threading the mazy paths of metaphysics, I had so placed myself in my arm-chair, that its front legs being raised about two inches from the floor, I was able, by balancing myself from left to right, to make way by degrees, and at last, almost without knowing it, to get close to the wall, for this is how I travel when not pressed for time. When there, my hand possessed itself by a mere mechanical effort, of the portrait of Madame de Haut-castel; and the OTHER amused itself with removing the dust which covered it. This occupation produced a feeling of quiet pleasure, and the pleasure was conveyed to my soul, lost though it was in the vast plains of heaven. For it is well to observe that when the mind is thus travelling in space, it still keeps linked to the senses by a secret and subtle chain; so that, without being distracted from its occupations, it can participate in the peaceful joys of the OTHER. But should this pleasure reach a certain pitch, or should the soul be struck by some unexpected vision, it forthwith descends swift as lightning, and resumes its place.

And that is just what happened to me while dusting the picture. Whilst the cloth removed the dust, and brought to

light those flaxen curls and the wreaths of
roses that crowned them, my soul, from the
sun, whither she had transported herself,
felt a slight thrill of pleasure, and partook
sympathetically of the joy of my heart.
This joy became less indistinct and more
lively, when, by a single sweep, the beautiful forehead of that. charming face was
revealed. My soul was on the point of
leaving the skies in order to enjoy the spectacle. But had she been in the Elysian
Fields, had she been engaged in a seraphic
concert, she could not have stayed a single
second longer when her companion, glow-
ing with the work, seized a proffered
sponge, and passed it at once over the eye-
brows and the eyes, over the nose, over
that mouth, ah heavens ! — my heart beats
at the thought — over the chin and neck !
It was the work of an instant. The whole
face .seemed suddenly recalled into existence. My soul precipitated herself like a

falling star from the sky. She found the
OTHER in a state of ecstasy, which she herself increased by sharing it. This strange
and unexpected position caused all thought
of time and space to vanish from my mind.
I lived for a moment in the past, and, contrary to the order of nature, I grew young
again. Yes, before me stands that adored
one ; 'tis she, her very self! She smiles
on me, she will speak and own her love.
That glance! . . . . come, let me press
thee to my heart, O, my loved one, my other
self! Partake with me this intoxicating
bliss! The moment was short, but ravishing. Cool reason soon reasserted her sway,
and in the twinkling of an eye I had grown a
whole year older. My heart grew icy cold,
and I found myself on a level with the
crowd of heedless ones who throng the
earth.

XI

Rose and White.

BUT we must not anticipate events. My hurry to communicate to the reader my system of the soul and animal caused me to abandon the description of my bed earlier than I ought to have done. When I have completed this description, I will continue my journey where I interrupted it in the last chapter. But let me pray you to bear in mind that we left one half of my *ego* four steps from my bureau, close to the wall, and holding the portrait of Madame de Hautcastel.

In speaking of my bed, I forgot to recommend every man to have, if possible, a bed with rose and white furniture. There can be no doubt that colors so far affect us as to make us cheerful or sad, according to their hues. Now, rose and white are two colors that are consecrated to pleasure. Nature in bestowing them upon the rose has given her the crown of Flora's realm. And when the sky would announce to the world a fine day, it paints the clouds at sunrise with this charming tint.

One day we were with some difficulty climbing a steep pathway. The amiable Rosalie, whose agility had given her wings, was far in front. We could not overtake her. All on a sudden, having reached the top of a hillock, she turned toward us to take breath, and smiled at our slowness. Never, perhaps, did the two colors whose praise I proclaim so triumph. Her burning cheeks, her coral lips, her alabaster neck, were thrown into relief by the verdure around, and entranced us all. We could not but pause and gaze upon her. I will not speak of her blue eyes, or of the glance she cast upon us, because this would be going from the subject, and because I dwell upon these memories as little as possible. Let it suffice that I have given the best illustration conceivable of the superiority of these two colors over all others, and of their influence upon the happiness of man.

Here will I stop for to-day. Of what subject can I treat which would not now be insipid? What idea is not effaced by *this* idea? I do not even know when I shall be able to resume my work. If I go on with it at all, and if the reader desire to see its termination, let him betake himself to the angel who distributes thoughts, and beg him to cease to mingle with the disconnected thoughts he showers upon me at every moment the image of that hillock.

If this precaution is not taken, my journey will be a failure.

XII.

The Hillock.

.   .   .   .   .   .

.   .   .   .   .   .

.   .   .   .   .   .

VEYSSILA D.   GUILLAUME S.

XIII.

A Halt.

MY efforts are useless. I must sojourn here awhile, whether I will or not. The " Halt !" is irresistible.

XIV.

Joannetti.

I REMARKED that I was singularly fond of meditating when influenced by the agreeable warmth of my bed ; and that its agreeable color added not a little to the pleasure I experienced.

That I may be provided with this enjoyment, my servant is directed to enter my room half an hour before my time for rising. I hear him moving about my room with a light step, and stealthily managing his preparations. This noise just suffices to convey to me the pleasant knowledge that I am slumbering, — a delicate pleasure this, unknown to most men. You are just awake enough to know you are not entirely so, and to make a dreamy calculation that

the hour for business and worry is still in
the sand-glass of time. Gradually my man
grows noisier; it is so hard for him to re-
strain himself, and he knows too that the
fatal hour draws near. He looks at my
watch, and jingles the seals as a warning.
But I turn a deaf ear to him. There is no
imaginable cheat I do not put upon the
poor fellow to lengthen the blissful moment. I give him a hundred preliminary
orders. He knows that these orders, given
somewhat peevishly, are mere excuses for
my staying in bed without seeming to wish
to do so. But this he affects not to see
through, and I am truly thankful to him.

At last, when I have exhausted all my
resources, he advances to the middle of the
room, and with folded arms, plants himself
there in a perfectly immovable position.
It must be admitted that it would be impossible to show disapproval of my idleness
with greater judgment and address. I

never resist this tacit invitation, but, stretching out my arms to show I understand him, get up at once.

If the reader will reflect upon the behavior of my servant, he will convince himself that in certain delicate matters of this kind, simplicity and good sense are much better than the sharpest wit. I dare assert that the most studied discourse on the impropriety of sloth would not make me spring so readily from my bed as the silent reproach of Monsieur Joannetti.

This Monsieur Joannetti is a thoroughly honest fellow, and at the same time just the man for such a traveller as I. He is accustomed to the frequent journeys of my soul, and never laughs at the inconsistencies of the OTHER. He even directs it occasionally when it is alone, so that one might say it is then conducted by two souls. When it is dressing, for instance, he will warn it by a gesture that it is on the point of putting on its stockings the wrong way, or its coat before its waistcoat.

Many a time has my soul been amused at seeing poor Joannetti running after this foolish creature under the arches of the citadel, to remind it of a forgotten hat or handkerchief. One day, I must confess, had it not been for this faithful servant, who caught it up just at the bottom of the staircase, the silly creature would have presented itself at court without a sword, as boldly as if it had been the chief gentleman-usher, bearing the august rod.

XV.

A Difficulty.

"COME, Joannetti," I said, "hang up this picture." He had helped to clean it, and had no more notion than the man in the moon what had produced our chapter on the portrait. He it was, who, of his own accord, held out the wet sponge, and who, through that seemingly unimportant act, caused my soul to travel a hundred millions of leagues in a moment of time. Instead of restoring it to its place, he held it to examine it in his turn. A difficulty, a problem, gave him an inquisitive air, which I did not fail to observe.

"Well, and what fault do you find with that portrait?" said I.

"O, none at all, sir."

" But come now, you have some remark to make, I know."

He placed it upright on one of the wings of my bureau, and then drawing back a little, " I wish, sir," he said, " that you would explain how it is that in whatever part of the room one may be, this portrait always watches you. In the morning, when I am making your bed, the face turns towards me; and if I move toward the window, it still looks at me, and follows me with its eyes as I go about."

" So that, Joannetti," said I, " if my room were full of people, that beautiful lady would eye every one, on all sides, at once."

" Just so, sir."

"She would smile on every comer and goer, just as she would on me ? "

Joannetti gave no further answer. I stretched myself in my easy-chair, and, hanging down my head, gave myself up to the most serious meditations. What a ray

of light fell upon me ! Alack, poor lover !
While thou pinest away, far from thy mistress, at whose side another perhaps, has
already replaced thee ; whilst thou fixest
thy longing eyes on her portrait, imagining
that at least in picture, thou art the sole
being she deigns to regard, — the perfidi-
ous image, as faithless as the original, be-
stows its glances on all around, and smiles
on every one alike !

And in this behold a moral resemblance
between certain portraits and their origi-
nals, which no philosopher, no painter, no
observer, had before remarked.

I go on from discovery to discovery.

VESSIER   GUILLAUME.

XVI.

Solution.

JOANNETTI remained in the attitude I
have described, awaiting the explanation
he had asked of me. I withdrew my head
from the folds of my travelling dress, into
which I had thrust it that I might meditate
more at my ease; and after a moment's
silence, to enable me to collect my thoughts
after the reflections I had just made, I said,
turning my arm-chair toward him, —

"Do you not see that as a picture is a
plane surface, the rays of light proceeding
from each point on that surface. . . . ?"

At that explanation, Joannetti stretched

his eyes to their very widest, while he kept his mouth half open. These two movements of the human face express, according to the famous Le Brun, the highest pitch of astonishment. It was, without doubt, my *animal*, that had undertaken this dissertation, while my soul was well aware that Joannetti knew nothing whatever about plane surfaces and rays of light. The prodigious dilatation of his eyelids caused me to draw back. I ensconced my head in the collar of my travelling coat, and this so effectively that I well-nigh succeeded in altogether hiding it. I determined to dine where I was. The morning was far advanced, and another step in my room would have delayed my dinner until night-fall. I let myself slip to the edge of my chair, and putting both feet on the mantel-piece, patiently awaited my meal. This was a most comfortable attitude ; indeed, it would be difficult to find another possessing so many advantages, and so well adapted to the inevitable sojourns of a long voyage.

At such moments, Rose, my faithful dog, never fails to come and pull at the skirts of my travelling dress that I may take her up. She finds a very convenient ready-made bed at the angle formed by the two parts of my body. A V admirably represents my position. Rose jumps to her post if I do not take her up quickly enough to please her, and I often find her there without knowing how she has come. My hands fall into a position which minister to her well-being, and this, either through a sympathy existing between this good-natured creature and myself, or through the merest chance. But no, I do not believe in that miserable doctrine of *chance*, — in that unmeaning word! I would rather believe in animal magnetism.

There is such reality in the relations which exist between these two animals,

that when out of sheer distraction, I put
my two feet on the mantel-piece and have
no thought at all about a *halt*, dinner-time
not being near, Rose, observing this movement, shows by a slight wag of her tail the
pleasure she enjoys. Reserve keeps her in
her place. The *other* perceives this and is
gratified by it, though quite unable to reason upon its cause. And thus a mute dialogue is established between them, a pleasing interchange of sensations which could
not be attributed to simple chance.

XVII.

Rose.

DO not reproach me for the prolixity with which I narrate the details of my journey. This is the wont of travellers. When one sets out for the ascent of Mont Blanc, or to visit the yawning tomb of Empedocles, the minutest particulars are carefully described. The number of persons who formed the party, the number of mules, the quality of the food, the excellent appetite of the travellers, — everything, to the very stumbling of the quadrupeds, is carefully noted down for the instruction of the sedentary world.

Upon this principle, I resolved to speak of my dog Rose, — an amiable creature for

4

whom I entertain sincere regard, — and to devote a whole chapter to her.

We have lived together for six years, and there has never been any coolness between us, and if ever any little disputes have arisen, the fault has been chiefly on my side, and Rose has always made the first advances towards reconciliation.

In the evening, if she has been scolded she withdraws sadly and without a murmur. The next morning at daybreak, she stands near my bed in a respectful attitude, and at her master's slightest movement, at the first sign of his being awake, she makes her presence known by rapidly tapping my little table with her tail.

And why should I refuse my affection to this good-natured creature that has never ceased to love me ever since we have lived together? My memory would not enable me to enumerate all the people who have interested themselves in me but to forget me. I have had some few friends, several lady-loves, a host of acquaintances ; and now I am to all these people as if I had never lived ; they have forgotten my very name.

And yet what protestations they made, what offers of assistance ! Their purse was at my disposal, and they begged me to depend upon their eternal and entire friendship !

Poor Rose, who has made me no promises, renders me the greatest service that can be bestowed upon humanity, for she has always loved her master, and loves him still. And this is why I do not hesitate to say that she shares with my other friends the affection I feel towards them.

XVIII.

.*Reserve.*

WE left Joannetti standing motionless before me, in an attitude of astonishment, awaiting the conclusion of the sublime explanation I had begun.

When he saw me bury my head in my dressing-gown, and thus end my dissertation, he did not doubt for a moment that I had stopped short for lack of resources, and that he had fairly overcome me by the knotty question he had plied me with.

Notwithstanding the superiority he had hereby gained over me, he felt no movement of pride, and did not seek to profit by his advantage. After a moment's silence, he took the picture, put it back in its place, and withdrew softly on tip-toe. He felt that his presence was a sort of humiliation to me, and his delicacy of feeling led him thus to retire unobserved. His behavior on this occasion interested me greatly, and gave him a higher place than ever in my affections. And he will have too, without doubt, a place in the heart of my readers. If there be one among them who will refuse it him after reading the next chapter, such a one must surely have a heart of stone.

XIX.

A Tear.

"GOOD Heavens!" said I to him one day, "three times have I told you to buy me a brush. What a head the fellow has!" He answered not a word; nor had he the evening before made any reply to a like expostulation. "This is very odd," I thought to myself, "he is generally so very particular."

"Well, go and get a duster to wipe my shoes with," I said angrily. While he was on his way, I regretted that I had spoken so sharply, and my anger entirely subsided when I saw how carefully he tried to remove the dust from my shoes without touching my stockings. "What," I said to myself, "are there then men who brush others' shoes for *money !*" This word *money* came upon me like a flash of lightning. I suddenly remembered that for a long time my servant had not had any money from me.

" Joannetti," said I, drawing away my foot, "have you any change?"

A smile of justification lit up his face at the question.

" No, sir ; for the last week I have not possessed a penny. I have spent all I had for your little purchases."

"And the brush ? I suppose that is why · .   .   .   ?"

He still smiled. Now, he might very well have said, " No, sir ; I am not the empty-headed ass you would make out your faithful servant to be. Pay me the one pound two shillings and sixpence halfpenny you owe me, and then I'll buy you your brush." But no, he bore this ill treatment rather than cause his master to blush at his unjust anger.   And may Heaven bless him !   Philosophers, Christians ! have you read this ?

"Come, Joannetti," said I, "buy me the brush."

"But, sir, will you go like that, with one shoe clean, and the other dirty ? "

"Go, go !" I replied, "never mind about the dust, never mind that."

He went out.   I took the duster, and daintily wiped my left shoe, on which a tear of repentance had fallen.

XX.

Albert and Charlotte.

THE walls of my room are hung with engravings and pictures, which adorn it greatly. I should much like to submit them to the reader's inspection, that they might amuse him along the road we have to traverse before we reach my bureau. But it is as impossible to describe a picture well, as to paint one from a description.

What an emotion he would feel in contemplating the first drawing that presents itself! He would see the unhappy Charlotte,[1] slowly, and with a trembling hand, wiping Albert's pistols. Dark forebodings, and all the agony of hopeless, inconsolable love, are imprinted on her features, while

[1] Vide *Werther*, chapter xxviii.

the cold-hearted Albert, surrounded by bags of law papers and various old documents, turns with an air of indifference towards his friend to bid him good-by. Many a time have I been tempted to break the glass that covers this engraving, that I might tear Albert away from the table, rend him to pieces, and trample him under foot. But this would not do away with the Alberts. There will always be sadly too many of them in the world. What sensitive man is there who has not such a one near him, who receives the overflowings of his soul, the gentle emotions of his heart, and the flights of his imagination just as the rock receives the waves of the sea? Happy is he who finds a friend whose heart and mind harmonize with his own; a friend who adheres to him by likeness of tastes, feeling, and knowledge; a friend who is not the prey of ambition or greediness, who prefers the shade of a tree to the pomp of a court! Happy is he who has a friend!

XXI.

A Friend.

I HAD a friend. Death took him from me. He was snatched away at the beginning of his career, at the moment when his friendship had become a pressing need to my heart. We supported one another in the hard toil of war. We had but one pipe between us. We drank out of the same cup. We slept beneath the same tent. And, amid our sad trials, the spot where we lived together became to us a new father-land. I had seen him exposed to all the perils of a disastrous war. Death seemed to spare us to each other. His

deadly missives were exhausted around
my friend a thousand times over without
reaching him ; but this was but to make his
loss more painful to me. The tumult of
war, and the enthusiasm which possesses
the soul at the sight of danger might have
prevented his sighs from piercing my heart,
while his death would have been useful to
his country, and damaging to the enemy.
Had he died thus, I should have mourned
him less. But to lose him amid the joys of
our winter-quarters ; to see him die at the
moment when he seemed full of health, and
when our intimacy was rendered closer by
rest and tranquillity, — ah, this was a blow
from which I can never recover !

But his memory lives in my heart, and
there alone. He is forgotten by those who
surrounded him, and who have replaced
him. And this makes his loss the more
sad to me.

Nature, in like manner indifferent to the

fate of individuals, dons her green spring robe, and decks herself in all her beauty near the cemetery where he rests. The trees cover themselves with foliage, and intertwine their branches ; the birds warble under the leafy sprays ; the insects hum among the blossoms : everything breathes joy in this abode of death.

And in the evening, when the moon shines in the sky, and I am meditating in this sad place, I hear the grasshopper, hidden in the grass that covers the silent grave of my friend, merrily pursuing his unwearied song. The unobserved destruction of human beings, as well as all their misfortunes, are counted for nothing in the grand total of events.

The death of an affectionate man who breathes his last surrounded by his afflicted friends, and that of a butterfly killed in a flower's cup by the chill air of morning, are but two similar epochs in the course of nature.   Man is but a phantom, a shadow, a mere vapor that melts into the air.

But day-break begins to whiten the sky. The gloomy thoughts that troubled me vanish with the darkness, and hope awakens again in my heart.   No!   He who thus suffuses the east with light, has not made it to shine upon my eyes only to plunge me into the night of annihilation.   He who has spread out that vast horizon, who raised those lofty mountains whose icy tops the sun is even now gilding, is also He who made my heart to beat, and my mind to think.

No!   My friend is not annihilated. Whatever may be the barrier that separates us, I shall see him again.   My hopes are based on no mere syllogism.   The flight of an insect suffices to persuade me. And often the prospect of the surrounding country, the perfume of the air, and an indescribable charm which is spread around me, so raise my thoughts, that an invincible proof of immortality forces itself upon my soul, and fills it to the full.

XXII.

Jenny.

THE chapter I have just written had often presented itself to my pen, but I had as often rejected it. I had promised myself that I would only allow the cheerful phase of my soul to show itself in this book. But this project, like many others, I was forced to abandon. I hope the sensitive reader will pardon me for having asked his tears ; and if any one thinks I should have omitted this chapter, he can tear it from his copy, or even throw the whole book on the fire.

Enough for me, dear Jenny, that thy heart approves it, thou best and best-beloved of women, best and best-beloved of sisters. To thee I dedicate my work. If it please thee, it will please all gentle and delicate hearts. And if thou wilt pardon the follies into which, albeit against my will, I sometimes fall, I will brave all the critics of the universe.

5

XXIII.

The Picture Gallery.

ONE word only upon our next engraving.

It represents the family of the unfortunate Ugolino, dying of hunger. Around him are his sons. One of them lies motionless at his feet. The rest stretch their enfeebled arms towards him, asking for bread ; while the wretched father, leaning against a pillar of his prison, his eyes fixed and haggard, his countenance immovable, dies a double death, and suffers all that human nature can endure.

And there is the brave Chevalier d'Assas, dying, by an effort of courage and heroism unknown in our days, under a hundred bayonets.

And thou who weepest under the palm-trees, poor negro woman! thou, whom some barbarous fellow has betrayed and deserted, nay, worse, whom he has had the brutality to sell as a vile slave, notwithstanding thy love and devotion, notwithstanding the pledge of affection thou hast borne at thy breast, — I will not pass before thine image without rendering to thee the homage due to thy tenderness and thy sorrows.

Let us pause a moment before the other picture. It is a young shepherdess tending her flock alone on the heights of the Alps. She sits on an old willow trunk, bleached by many winters. Her feet are covered by the broad leaves of a tuft of *cacalia*, whose lilac blossoms bloom above her head. Lavender, wild thyme, the anemone, centaury, and flowers which are cultivated with care in our hot-houses and gardens, and which grow in all their native beauty on the Alps, form the gay carpet on which her sheep wander.

Lovely shepherdess! tell me where is the lovely spot thou callest thy home. From what far-off sheepfold didst thou set out at daybreak this morning? Could I not go thither and live with thee?

But alas, the sweet tranquillity thou enjoyest will soon vanish! The demon of war, not content with desolating cities, will ere long carry anxiety and alarm to thy solitary retreat. Even now I see the soldiers advancing: they climb height after height, as they march upward towards the clouds. The cannons' roar is heard high above the thunder-clap.

Fly, O shepherdess! Urge on thy flock! Hide thee in the farthest caves, for no longer is repose to be found on this sad earth!

XXIV.

Painting and Music.

I DO not know how it is, but of late my chapters have always ended in a mournful strain. In vain do I begin by fixing my eyes on some agreeable object ; in vain do I embark when all is calm : a sudden gale soon drifts me away. To put an end to an agitation which deprives me of the mastery of my ideas, and to quiet the beating of a heart too much disturbed by so many touching images, I see no remedy but a dissertation. Yes, thus will I steel my heart.

And the dissertation shall be about painting, for I cannot at this moment expatiate upon any other subject. I cannot altogether descend from the point I just now reached. Besides, painting is to me what Uncle Toby's hobby-horse was to him.[1]

I would say a few words, by the way, upon the question of preëminence between the charming arts of painting and music. I would cast my grain into the balance, were it but a grain of sand, a mere atom.

It is urged in favor of the painter, that he leaves his works behind him ; that his pictures outlive him, and immortalize his memory.

In reply to this we are reminded that musical composers also leave us their operas and oratorios.

But music is subject to fashion, and painting is not. The musical passages that deeply affected our forefathers seem

---

[1] The reader will probably have been reminded of the "Sentimental Journey" before reaching this proof of our author's acquaintance with the writings of Sterne.

H. A.

simply ridiculous to the amateurs of our own day; and they are placed in absurd farces to furnish laughter for the nephews of those whom they once made to weep.

Raphael's pictures will enchant our descendants as greatly as they did our forefathers.

This is my grain of sand.

XXV

An Objection.

"BUT what," said Madame de Haut-castel to me one day, — "what if the music of Cherubini or Cimarosa differs from that of their predecessors? What care I if the music of the past make me laugh, so long as that of the present day touch me by its charms? Is it at all essential to my happiness that my pleasures should resemble those of my great-grandmother? Why talk to me of painting, an art which is only enjoyed by a very small class of persons, while music enchants every living creature?"

I hardly know at this moment how one could reply to this observation, which I did not foresee when I began my chapter.

Had I foreseen it, perhaps I should not have undertaken that dissertation. And pray do not imagine that you discover in this *objection* the artifice of a musician, for upon my honor I am none, Heaven be my witness, and all those who have heard me play the violin !

But, even supposing the merits of the two arts to be equal, we must not be too hasty in concluding that the merits of the *disciples* of Painting and Music are therefore balanced. We see children play the harpsichord as if they were *maestri*, but no one has ever been a good painter at twelve years old. Painting, besides taste and feeling, requires an amount of thoughtfulness that musicians can dispense with. Any day may you hear men who are well nigh destitute of head and heart, bring out from a violin or harp the most ravishing sounds.

The human ANIMAL may be taught to play the harpsichord, and when it has learned of a good master, the soul can travel at her ease while sounds with which she does not concern herself are mechanically produced by the fingers. But the simplest thing in the world cannot be painted without the aid of all the faculties of the soul.

If, however, any one should take it into his head to ply me with a distinction between the composition and the performance of music, I confess that he would give me some little difficulty. Ah, well! were all writers of essays quite candid they would all conclude as I am doing. When one enters upon the examination of a question, a dogmatic tone is generally assumed, because there has been a secret decision beforehand, just as I, notwithstanding my hypocritical impartiality, had decided in favor of painting. But discussion awakens objections, and everything ends with doubt.

XXVI.

Raphael.

NOW that I am more tranquil, I will endeavor to speak calmly of the two portraits that follow the picture of the shepherdess of the Alps.

Raphael! Who but thyself could paint thy portrait ; who but thyself would have dared attempt it ? Thy open countenance, beaming with feeling and intellect, proclaims thy character and thy genius.

To gratify thy shade, I have placed beside thee the portrait of thy mistress, whom the men of all generations will hold answerable for the loss of the sublime works of which art has been deprived by thy premature death.

When I examine the portrait of Raphael,

I feel myself penetrated by an almost religious respect for that great man, who, in the flower of his age, excelled the ancients, and whose pictures are at once the admiration and the despair of modern artists. My soul, in admiring it, is moved with indignation against that Italian who preferred her love to her lover, and who extinguished at her bosom that heavenly flame, that divine genius.   .

Unhappy one! Knewest thou not that Raphael had announced a picture superior even to that of the *Transfiguration?* Didst thou not know that thine arms encircled the favorite of nature, the father of enthusiasm, a sublime genius. . . . a divinity ?

While my soul makes these observations, her companion, whose eyes are attentively fixed upon the lovely face of that fatal beauty, feels quite ready to forgive her the death of Raphael.

In vain my soul upbraids this extravagant weakness ; she is not listened to at all. On such occasions a strange dialogue arises between the two, which terminates too often in favor of the bad principles, and of which I reserve a sample for another chapter.

And if, by the way, my soul had not at that moment abruptly closed the inspection of the gallery, if she had given the OTHER time to contemplate the rounded and graceful features of the beautiful Roman lady, my intellect would have miserably lost its supremacy.

And if, at that critical moment I had suddenly obtained the favor bestowed upon the fortunate Pygmalion, without having the least spark of the genius which makes me pardon Raphael his errors, it is just possible that I should have succumbed as he did.

XXVII.

A Perfect Picture.

MY engravings, and the paintings of which I have spoken, fade away into nothing at the first glance bestowed upon the next picture. The immortal works of Raphael and Correggio, and of the whole Italian school, are not to be compared to it. Hence it is that when I accord to an amateur the pleasure of travelling with me, I always keep this until the last as a special luxury, and ever since I first exhibited this sublime picture to connoisseurs and to ignorant, to men of the world, to artists, to women, to children, to animals even, I have always found the spectators, whoever they might be, show, each in his own way, signs of pleasure and surprise, so admirably is nature rendered therein.

And what picture could be presented to you, gentlemen ; what spectacle, ladies, could be placed before your eyes more certain of gaining your approval than the faithful portraiture of yourselves? The picture of which I speak is a mirror, and no one has as yet ventured to criticise it. It is to all who look on it a perfect picture, in depreciation of which not a word can be said.

You will at once admit that it should be regarded as one of the wonders of the world.

I will pass over in silence the pleasure felt by the natural philosopher in meditating upon the strange phenomena presented by light as it reproduces upon that polished. surface all the objects of nature. A mirror offers to the sedentary traveller a thousand interesting reflections, a thousand observations which render it at once a useful and precious article.

Ye whom Love has held or still holds under his sway, learn that it is before a mirror that he sharpens his darts, and contemplates his cruelties. There it is that he plans his manœuvres, studies his tactics, and prepares himself for the war he wishes to declare. There he practices his killing glances and little affectations, and sly poutings, just as a player practices, with himself for spectator, before appearing in public.

A mirror, being always impartial and true, brings before the eyes of the beholder the roses of youth and the wrinkles of age, without calumny and without flattery. It alone among the councilors of the great, invariably tells them the truth.

It was this recommendation that made me desire the invention of a moral mirror, in which all men might see themselves, with their virtues and their vices. I even thought of offering a prize to some academy for this discovery, when riper reflection proved to me that such an invention would be useless.

Alas ! how rare it is for ugliness to recognize itself and break the mirror! In vain are looking-glasses multiplied around us which reflect light and truth with geometrical exactness. As soon as the rays reach our vision and paint us as we are, self-love slips its deceitful prism between us and our image, and presents a divinity to us.

And of all the prisms that have existed since the first that came from the hands of the immortal Newton, none has possessed so powerful a refractive force, or produced such pleasing and lively colors, as the prism of self-love.

Now, seeing that ordinary looking-glasses record the truth in vain, and that they cannot make men see their own imperfections, every one being satisfied with his face, what would a moral mirror avail?

Few people would look at it, and no one would recognize himself. None save philosophers would spend their time in examining themselves, — I even have my doubts about the philosophers.

Taking the mirror as we find it, I hope no one will blame me for ranking it above all the pictures of the Italian school.

Ladies, whose taste cannot be faulty, and whose opinion should decide the question, generally upon entering a room let their first glance fall upon this picture.

A thousand times have I seen ladies, aye, and gallants, too, forget at a ball their lovers and their mistresses, the dancing, and all the pleasures of the fete, to contemplate with evident complaisance this enchanting picture, and honoring it even, from time to time, in the midst of the liveliest quadrille, with a look.

Who then can dispute the rank that I accord to it among the masterpieces of the art of Apelles?

XXVIII.

The Upset Carriage.

I HAD at last nearly reached my bureau.
So close was I, that had I stretched out
my arm I could have touched the corner
nearest to me. But at this very moment I
was on the verge of seeing the fruit of all
my labors destroyed, and of losing my life.
I should pass over in silence the accident
that happened to me, for fear of discourag-
ing other travellers, were it not that it is so
difficult to upset such a post-chaise as I
employ, that it must be allowed that one
must be uncommonly unlucky — as unlucky, indeed, as it is my lot to be — to be
exposed to a like danger.

There I was, stretched at full length
upon the ground, completely upset, and it

was done so quickly, so unexpectedly, that
I should have been almost tempted to
question the cause of my abject position,
had not a singing in my ears and a sharp
pain in my left shoulder too plainly demon-
strated it.

This was again the OTHER, who had
played a trick upon me.

Startled by the voice of a poor man who
suddenly asked alms at my door, and by
the voice of Rose, my other half suddenly
turned the arm-chair sharply round, before
my soul had time to warn it that a piece of
brick, which served as a drag, was gone.
The jerk was so violent that my post-
chaise was quite thrown from its centre of
gravity, and turned over upon me.

This was, I must own, one of the occasions upon which I had most to complain
of my soul. For instead of being vexed
at herself for having been absent, and
scolding her companion for its hurry, she

so far forgot herself as to give way to the most animal resentment, and to insult the poor fellow cruelly.

"Idle rascal," she said, "go and work." (An execrable apostrophe this, the invention of miserly, heartless Mammon.)

"Sir," replied the man, hoping to soften my heart, "I come from Chambéry."

"So much the worse for you."

"I am James. You saw me when you were in the country. I used to drive the sheep into the fields."

"And what do you do here?" My soul began to regret the harshness of my first words; I almost think she regretted them a moment before they were uttered. In like manner, when one meets in the road a rut or puddle, one sees it, but has not time to avoid it.

Rose finished the work of bringing me to good sense and repentance. She had recognized Jem, who had often shared his crust with her, and she testified by her caresses, her remembrance and gratitude.

Meanwhile, Joannetti, who had gathered together what was left of my dinner, his own share, gave it at once to Jem.

Poor Joannetti !

Thus it is that in my journey I get lessons of philosophy and humanity from my servant and my dog.

XXIX.

Misfortune.

BEFORE proceeding farther, I wish to remove a suspicion which may have crossed the minds of my readers.

I would not for all the world be suspected of having undertaken this journey just because I did not know how to spend my time, and was in a manner compelled thereto by circumstances. I here affirm, and swear by all that is dear to me, that I projected it long before the event took place which deprived me of my liberty for forty-two days. This forced retirement only served as an opportunity for setting out sooner than I had intended.

This gratuitous protestation will, I know, appear suspicious in the eyes of some.

But those who are so ready to suspect are just the persons who will not read this book. They have enough to do at home and at their friends', plenty of other business to attend to. And good, honest folk will believe me.

Still, I freely admit that I should have preferred another season for my journey, and that I should have chosen for its execution Lent rather than the Carnival. The philosophical reflections, however, that have come to me from above have greatly aided me in supporting the loss of those pleasures which Turin offers at this noisy and exciting time.

It is certain, I have thought to myself, that the walls of my chamber are not so magnificently decorated as those of a ballroom. The silence of my cottage is far less agreeable than the pleasing sounds of music and dancing. But among the brilliant personages one meets in those fes-

tive scenes, there are certainly some who
are more sick at heart than I am.

And why should I picture to myself
those who are more happily circumstanced
than it is my lot to be, while the world
swarms with those who are worse off? Instead of transporting myself in fancy to that
sumptuous dancing-hall, where so many
beauties are eclipsed by the young Eugénie,
I need only pause a moment in one of the
streets, that lead thither, if I would learn
how happy is my fate.

For, under the porticos of those magnifi-
cent apartments, lie a crowd of wretched
people, half-naked, and ready to die from
cold and misery. What a spectacle is
here! Would that this page of my book
were known throughout the universe!
Would that every one knew that in this
opulent city a host of wretched beings
sleep, without covering, in the coldest winter nights, and with no pillow but the

corner-stone of a street, or the steps of a palace.

Here, again, is a group of children, crouching together for protection from the deadly cold ; and here a trembling woman, who has no voice left to complain with: The passers-by come and go without being touched by a spectacle with which they are so familiar. The noise of carriages, the shouts of intemperance, the ravishing sounds of music, mingle not unfrequently with the wails of those unhappy creatures, and fill the ear with doleful discord.

XXX.

Charity.

WERE any one to pass a hasty judgment upon a city, taking my last chapter as a criterion, he would err greatly. I have spoken of the poor we meet with, of their pitiful lamentations, and of the indifference with which many regard them. But I have said nothing of the multitude of charitable persons who sleep while others seek amusement, and who rise at dawn, unobserved and unostentatiously, to succor the unfortunate.

This aspect of city life must not be passed by in silence. I will write it on the reverse of the page I was anxious everybody should read.

After having divided their good things

with their brethren, after having poured balm into hearts chafed by sorrow, you may see them enter the churches, while wearied vice sleeps upon eider-down, to offer up. their prayers to God, and to thank Him for his mercies. The light of a solitary lamp still struggles in the sanctuary with the daylight; but they are already prostrate before the altar. And the Almighty, angered by the hard-hearted selfishness of men, witholds his threatening hand.

XXXI.

Inventory.

I COULD not help saying a word in my journey about those poor creatures, for the thought of them has often come across me on my way, and turned the current of my reflections. Sometimes, struck with the difference between their case and my own, I have suddenly stopped my travelling-carriage, and thought my chamber extravagantly embellished ! What superfluous luxury ! Six chairs, two tables, a bureau, and a looking-glass ! What vain display ! My bed above all things, my rose and white bed, with its two mattresses, seemed to rival the magnificence and effeminacy of Asiatic monarchs.

These meditations made me indifferent

to the pleasures that had been forbidden me. And, as I went on from one reflection to another, my fit of philosophy became so serious that I could have seen a ball going on in the next room, and heard the sound of violins and flutes without stirring. I could have heard Marchesini's melodious voice, that voice which has so often transported me, yes, I could have listened to it without being moved. Nay, more, I could have gazed upon the most beauteous woman in Turin, upon Eugénie herself, adorned from head to foot by the hands of Mademoiselle Rapoux,[1] without emotion. But, of this last, I must confess myself not quite sure.

[1] A fashionable milliner of the time.

XXXII.

Misanthropy.

BUT, gentlemen, allow me to ask a question. Do you enjoy balls and plays as much as you used to do? As for me, I avow that for some time past crowded assemblies have inspired me with a kind of terror. When in their midst, I am assailed by an ominous dream. In vain I try to shake it off; like the dream of *Athalie*, it constantly returns. Perhaps this is because the soul, overwhelmed at the present moment by dark fancies and painful pictures, sees nothing but sadness around it, just as a disordered stomach turns the most wholesome food into poison. However this may be, my dream is as follows. When I am at one of these fêtes, among a crowd of kind, good-natured men, who dance and sing, who weep at tragedies, and are full of frankness and cordiality, I say to myself : —

"If suddenly a white bear, a philosopher, a tiger, or some other animal of this kind were to enter, and ascending to the orchestra, were to shout out furiously : 'Wretched beings! Listen to the truth that comes from my lips! You are oppressed! You are the slaves of tyrants! You are wretched and heart-sick! Awake from your lethargy!

"'Musicians, break your instruments about your heads, and let each one of you arm himself with a poniard. Think no more about holidays and rejoicings. Climb into the boxes, and stab their occupants, one and all. And let the women steep their timid hands in blood.

"'Quit this room, for you are free! Tear your king from his throne, and your God from his sanctuary.'

" Well, and how many of these charming men will obey this tiger's voice. How
many of them thought, perhaps, of such
deeds before they entered ? Who can
tell ? Was there no dancing in Paris five
years ago ? "

Joannetti ! shut the door and windows !
I do not wish to see the light ! Let no
one enter my room. Put my sword within
reach. Go out yourself, and keep away
from me.

7

XXXIII.

Consolation.

NO, no! Stay, Joannetti, my good fellow! And you too, Rose, you who guess what are my sorrows, and soften them by your caresses, come!

V forms the resting-place.

XXXIV.

Correspondence.

THE upset of my post-chaise has rendered the reader the service of shortening my journey by a good dozen chapters, for, upon getting up, I found myself close to my bureau, and saw that I had no time left for any observations upon a number of engravings and pictures which had yet to be surveyed, and which might have lengthened my excursions into the realm of painting.

Leaving to the right the portraits of Raphael and his mistress, the Chevalier d'Assas and the Shepherdess of the Alps, and taking the left, the side on which the window is situated, my bureau comes into view. It is the first and the most prominent object the traveller's eyes light upon, taking the route I have indicated.

It is surmounted by a few shelves that serve as a book-case, and the whole is terminated by a bust which completes the pyramid, and contributes more than any other object to the adornment of this region.

Upon opening the first drawer to the left, we find an inkstand, paper of all kinds, pens ready mended, and sealing-wax; all which set the most indolent person longing to write.

I am sure, dear Jenny, that if you chanced to open this drawer, you would reply to the letter I wrote you a year ago.

In the opposite drawer lies a confused heap of materials for a touching history of the prisoner of Pignerol,[1] which, my dear friends, you will ere long read.

Between these two drawers is a recess

[1] This work was not published.

into which I throw whatever letters I receive. All that have reached me during the last ten years are there. The oldest of them are arranged according to date in several packets ; the new ones lie pell-mell. Besides these, I have several dating from my early boyhood.

How great a pleasure it is to behold again through the medium of these letters the interesting scenes of our early years, to be once again transported into those happy days that we shall see no more !

How full is my heart, and how deeply tinged with sadness is its joy, as my eyes wander over those words traced by one who is gone forever ! That handwriting is his, and it was his heart that guided his hand. It was to me that he addressed this letter, and this letter is all that is left of him !

When I put my hand into this recess, I seldom leave the spot for the whole day.

In like manner, a traveller will pass rapidly through whole provinces of Italy, making a few hurried and trivial observations on the way, and upon reaching Rome will take up his abode there for months.

This is the richest vein in the mine I am exploring. How changed I find my ideas and sentiments, and how altered do my friends appear when I examine them as they were in days gone by, and as they are now! In these mirrors of the past I see them in mortal agitation about plans which no longer disturb them.

Here I find an event announced which we evidently looked upon as a great misfortune; but the end of the letter is wanting, and the circumstance is so entirely forgotten that I cannot now make out what the matter was which so concerned us. We were possessed by a thousand prejudices. We knew nothing of the world, and of men. But then, how warm was our intercourse!

How intimate our friendship! How unbounded our confidence!

In our ignorance there was bliss. But now, — ah! all is now changed. We have been compelled, as others, to read the human heart; and truth, falling like a bomb into the midst of us, has forever destroyed the enchanted palace of illusion.

XXXV.

The Withered Rose.

I F the subject were worth the trouble, I could readily write a chapter upon that dry rose. It is a flower of last year's carnival. I gathered it myself in the Valentino.[1] And in the evening, an hour before the ball was to begin, I bore it, full of hope, and agreeably excited, to Madame Hautcastel, for her acceptance. She took it, and without looking at it or me, placed it upon her toilette-table. And how could she have given *me* any of her attention? She was engaged in looking at herself.

[1] The botanical garden of Turin.

There she stood before a large mirror ; her hair was ornamented for a fête, and the decorations of her dress were undergoing their final arrangement. She was so fully occupied, her attention was so totally absorbed by the ribbons, gauzes, and all sorts of finery that lay in heaps before her, that I did not get a look or any sign of recognition. There was nothing for me but resignation. I held out humbly in my hand a number of pins arranged in order. But her pincushion being more within reach, she took them from her pincushion, and when I brought my hand nearer, she took them from my hand, quite indifferently, and in taking them up she would feel about for them with the tips of her fingers, without taking her eyes from the glass, lest she should lose sight of herself.

For some time I held behind her a second mirror that she might judge the better how her dress became her, and as her face reflected itself from one glass to another, I saw a prospective of coquettes, no one of whom paid me the least attention. In a word, I must confess that my rose and I cut a very poor figure.

At last I lost all patience, and unable longer to control the vexation that preyed upon me, I put down the looking-glass I had been holding, and went out angrily without taking leave.

"O! you are going?" she said, turning so as to see her figure in profile. I made no answer, but I listened some time at the door to see what effect my abrupt departure would have.

"Do you not see," she said to her maid, after a moment's silence, "that this caraco, particularly the lower part, is much too large at the waist, and will want pinning?"

Why and wherefore that rose is upon my shelf, I shall certainly not explain, for, as I said before, a withered rose does not deserve a chapter.

And pray observe, ladies, that I make no
reflection upon the adventure with the
rose. I do not say whether Madame de
Hautcastel did well or otherwise in prefer-
ring her dress to me, or whether I had any
right to a better reception.   .

I take special care to deduce therefrom
no general conclusions about the reality,
the strength, and the duration of the affection of ladies for their friends. I am content to cast this chapter (since it is one)
into the world with the rest of my journey,
without addressing it to any one, and without recommending it to any one.

·I will only add, gentlemen, a word of
counsel. Impress well upon your minds
this fact, that your mistress is no longer
yours on the day of a ball.

As soon as dressing begins, a lover is no
more thought of than a husband would be ;
and the ball takes the place of a lover.

Every one knows how little a husband

gains by enforcing his love. Take your trouble, then, patiently, cheerfully.

And, my dear sir, do not deceive yourself; if a lady welcome you at a ball, it is not as a lover that you are received, for you are a husband — but as a part of the ball; and you are therefore but a fraction of her new conquest. You are the decimal of a lover. Or, it may be, you dance well, and so give éclat to her graces. After all, perhaps, the most flattering way in which you can regard her kind welcome is to consider that she hopes by treating as her cavalier a man of parts like yourself, to excite the jealousy of her companions. Were it not for that she would not notice you at all.

It amounts then to this. You must resign yourself to your fate, and wait until the husband's *rôle* is played. I know those who would be glad to get off at so cheap a rate.

XXXVI.

The Library.

I PROMISED to give a dialogue between my soul and the OTHER. But there are some chapters which elude me, as it were, or rather, there are others which flow from my pen *nolens volens*, and derange my plans. Among these is one about my library; and I will make it as short as I can. Our forty-two days will soon be ended; and even were it not so, a similar period would not suffice to complete the description of the rich country in which I travel so pleasantly.

My library, then, is composed of novels, if I must make the confession ; of novels and a few choice poets.

As if I had not troubles enough of my

.

own, I share those of a thousand imaginary personages, and I feel them as acutely as my own. How many tears have I shed for that poor Clarissa,[1] and for Charlotte's [2] lover !

But if I go out of my way in search of unreal afflictions, I find in return, such virtue, kindness, and disinterestedness in this imaginary world as I have never yet found united in the real world around me. I meet with a woman after my heart's desire, free from whim, lightness, and affectation. I say nothing about beauty ; this I can leave to my imagination, and picture her faultlessly beautiful. And then, closing the book, which no longer keeps pace with my ideas, I take the fair one by the hand, and we travel together over a country a thousand times more delightful than Eden itself. What painter could represent the

[1] Richardson's *Clarissa Harlowe.*
[2] Goethe's *Werther.*

fairy land in which I have placed thè goddess of my heart? What poet could ever
describe the lively and manifold sensations
I experience in those enchanted regions ?

How often have I cursed that Cleveland,[1]
who is always embarking upon new troubles
which he might very well avoid! I cannot endure that book with its long list of
calamities. But if I open it by way of distraction, I cannot help devouring it to the
end.

For how could I leave that poor man
among the Abaquis ? What would become
of him in the hands of those savages ?
Still less dare I leave him in his attempt
to escape from captivity.

Indeed, I so enter into his sorrows, I am
so interested in him and in his unfortunate
family, that the sudden appearance of the
ferocious Ruintons makes my hair stand
on end. When I read that passage a cold

---

[1] *Cleveland,* by the Abbé Prévost.

perspiration covers me, and my fright is as lively and real as if I was going to be roasted and eaten by the monsters myself.

When I have had enough of tears and love, I turn to some poet, and set out again for a new world.

XXXVII.

Another World.

FROM the Argonautic expedition to the Assembly of Notables ; from the bottom of the nethermost pit to the furthest fixed star beyond the Milky Way ; to the confines of the Universe ; to the gates of chaos ; thus far extends the vast field over the length and breadth of which I leisurely roam. I lack nor time nor space. Thither, conducted by Homer, by Milton, by Virgil, by Ossian, I transport my existence.

All the events that have taken place between these two epochs ; all the countries, all the worlds, all the beings that have existed between these two boundaries, — all are mine, all as lawfully belong to me as the

8

ships that entered the Piræus belonged to a certain Athenian.

Above all the rest do I love the poets who carry me back to the remotest antiquity. The death of the ambitious Agamemnon, the madness of Orestes, and the tragical history of the heaven-persecuted family of the Atrides, inspire me with a terror that all the events of modern times could not excite in my breast.

Behold the fatal urn which contains the ashes of Orestes! Who would not shudder at the sight? Electra, unhappy sister! be comforted, for it is Orestes himself who bears the urn, and the ashes are those of his enemies.

No longer are their banks like those of Xanthus or the Scamander. No longer do we visit plains such as those of Hesperia or Arcadia. Where are now the isles of Lemnos and Crete? Where the famous labyrinth? Where is the rock that forlorn

Ariadne washed with her tears? Theseus is seen no more; Hercules is gone forever. The men, aye, and the heroes of our day are but pigmies.

When I would visit a scene full of enthusiasm, and put forth all the strength of my imagination, I cling boldly to the flowing robe of the sublime blind poet of Albion at the moment when he soars heavenward, and dares approach the throne of the Eternal. What muse was able to sustain him in a flight so lofty that no man before him ever ventured to raise his eyes so high? From heaven's dazzling pavement which avaricious Mammon looked down upon with envious eyes, I pass, horror-stricken, to the vast caverns of Satan's sojourn. I take my place at the infernal council, mingle with the host of rebellious spirits, and listen to their discourse.

But here I must confess a weakness for which I have often reproached myself.

I cannot help taking a certain interest in Satan, thus hurled headlong from heaven. (I am speaking, of course, of *Milton's* Satan.) While I blame the obstinacy of the rebel angel, the firmness he shows in the midst of his exceeding great misery, and the grandness of his courage, inspire me, against my will, with admiration. Although not ignorant of the woe resulting from the direful enterprise that led him to force the gate of hell and to trouble the home of our first parents, I cannot for a moment, do what I will, wish he may perish in the confusion of chaos on his way. I even think I could willingly help him, did not shame withhold me. I follow his every movement, and take as much pleasure in travelling with him as if I were in very good company. In vain I consider that after all he is a devil on his way to the ruin of the human race, that he is a thorough democrat, not after the manner of those of

Athens, but of Paris. All this does not cure me of my prejudice in his favor.

How vast was his project! How great the boldness displayed in its execution!

When the thrice-threefold gates of hell fly open before him, and the dark, boundless ocean discloses itself in all its horror at his feet, with undaunted eye he surveys the realm of chaos, and then, opening his sail-broad wings, precipitates himself into the abyss.[1]

To me this passage is one of the noblest efforts of imagination, and one of the most splendid journeys ever made, next to *the journey round my room.*

---

[1] Some freedom of translation is, perhaps, pardonable here. Our author, depending, it would seem, upon his memory, gives Satan wings large enough "to cover a whole army" It was "the extended wings" of the gates of hell, not of Satan, that Milton describes as wide enough to admit a "bannered host." *Paradise Lost*, ii. 885. H. A.

XXXVIII.

The Bust.

I SHOULD never end if I tried to describe a thousandth part of the strange events I meet with when I travel in my library. The voyages of Cook and the observations of his fellow-travellers Banks and Solander are nothing compared with my adventures in this one district. Indeed, I think I could spend my life there in a kind of rapture, were it not for the bust I have already mentioned, upon which my eyes and thoughts always fix themselves at last, whatever may be the position of my soul. And when my soul is violently agitated, or a prey to despair, a glance at this bust suffices to restore the troubled being to its natural state. It sounds the chord upon which I keep in tune the harmonies, and correct the discords of the sensations and perceptions of which my being is made up. How striking the likeness ! Those are the features nature gave to the best of men. O, that the sculptor had been able to bring to view his noble soul, his genius, his character ! But what am I attempting ! Is it here that his praise should be recorded ? Do I address myself to the men that surround me ? Ah ! what concern is it of theirs ?

I am contented to bend before thy image, O best of fathers ! Alas, that this should be all that is left me of thee and of my father-land ! Thou quittedst the earth when crime was about to invade it ; and so heavy are the ills that oppress thy family, that we are constrained to regard thy loss as a blessing. Many would have been the evils a longer life would have brought upon thee ! And dost thou, O my father, dost thou, in thine abode of bliss, know the lot of thy family! Knowest thou that thy children are exiled from the country thou hast served with so much zeal and integrity for sixty years?

Dost thou know that they are forbidden to visit thy grave? But tyranny has not been able to deprive them of the most precious part of thy heritage, the record of thy virtues, and the force of thine example. In the midst of the torrent of crime which has borne their father-land and their patrimony to ruin, they have steadfastly remained united in the path marked out for them by thee. And when it shall be given them to prostrate themselves once more beside thy tomb, thou shalt see in them thine obedient children.

XXXIX.

A Dialogue.

I PROMISED a dialogue, and I will keep my word.

It was daybreak. The rays of the sun were gilding the summit of Mount Viso, and the tops of the highest hills on the island beneath our feet. My soul was already awake. This early awakening may have been the effect of those night visions which often excite in her a fatiguing and useless agitation : or perhaps the carnival, then drawing to a close, was the secret cause ; for this season of pleasure and folly influences the human organization much as do the phases of the moon and the conjunction of certain planets. However this may be, my soul was awake, and wide awake, when she shook off the bands of sleep.

For some time she had shared, though confusedly, the sensations of the OTHER: but she was still encumbered by the swathes of night and sleep; and these swathes seemed to her transformed into gauze and fine linen and Indian lawn. My poor soul was, as it were, enwrapped in all this paraphernalia, and the god of sleep, that he might hold her still more firmly under his sway, added to these bonds disheveled tresses of flaxen hair, ribbon bows, and pearl necklaces. Really it was pitiful to see her struggle in these toils.

The agitation of the nobler part of myself communicated itself to the OTHER; and the latter, in its turn, reacted powerfully upon my soul.

I worked myself, at last, into a state which it would be hard to describe, while my soul, either sagaciously or by chance, hit upon a way of escaping from the gauzes by which it was being suffocated. I know

not whether she discovered an outlet, or
whether, which is a more natural conclusion, it occurred to her to raise them : at all
events, she found a means of egress from
the labyrinth. The tresses of disheveled
hair were still there ; but they were now
rather help than hindrance ; my soul seized
them, as a drowning man clutches the
sedge on a river's bank, but the pearl neck-
lace broke in the act, and the unstrung
pearls rolled on the sofa, and from the sofa,
to Madame Hautcastel's floor (for my soul,
by an eccentricity for which it would be
difficult to give a reason, fancied she was
at that lady's house) ; then a great bunch
of violets fell to the ground, and my soul,
which then awoke, returned home, bring-.
ing with her common sense and reality.
She strongly disapproved, as you will readily imagine, of all that had passed in her
absence ; and here it is that the dialogue
begins which forms the subject of this
chapter.

Never had my soul been so ungraciously received. The complaints she thought fit to make at this critical moment fully sufficed to stir up domestic strife ; a revolt, a formal insurrection followed.

"What !" said my soul, "is it thus that during my absence, instead of restoring your strength by quiet sleep that you may be better able to do my bidding, you have the insolence (the expressing was rather strong) to give yourself up to transports which my authority has not sanctioned !"

Little accustomed to this haughty tone, the OTHER angrily answered : —

"Really, madame" (this madame was meant to remove from the discussion anything like familiarity), "really, this affectation of virtuous decorum is highly becoming to you ! Is it not to the sallies of your imagination, and to your extravagant ideas, that I owe what in me displeases you ? What right have you to go on those pleasant excursions so often, without taking me with you? Have I ever complained about your attending the meetings in the Empyrean or in the Elysian fields, your conversations with the celestial intelligences, your profound speculations (a little raillery here, you see), your castles in the air, and your transcendental systems? And have I not a right, when you leave me in this way, to enjoy the blessings bestowed upon me by Nature, and the pleasures she places before me?"

My soul, surprised at so much vivacity and eloquence, did not know how to reply. In order to settle the dispute amicably, she endeavored to veil with the semblance of good-nature the reproaches that had escaped her. But, that she might not seem to take the first steps towards reconciliation, she affected a formal tone. "*Madame*," she said, with assumed cordiality. . . . . If the reader thought

the word misplaced when addressed to my
soul, what will he say of it now, if he call to
mind the cause of the quarrel ? But my soul
did not feel the extreme absurdity of this
mode of expression, so much does passion
obscure the intellect ! " Madame," she said,
" nothing, be assured, would give me so
much pleasure as to see you enjoy those
pleasures of which your nature is suscepti-
ble, if even I did not participate in them,
were it not that such pleasures are harmful
to you, injuriously affecting the harmony
which . . ." Here my soul was rudely
interrupted, " No, no, I am not the dupe of
your pretended kindness. The sojourn we
are compelled to make together in this room
in which we travel ; the wound which I received, which still bleeds, and which nearly
destroyed me, — is not all this the fruit of
your overweening conceit and your barbarous prejudices ? My comfort, my very existence, is counted as nothing when your

passions sway you : and then, forsooth, you
pretend that you take an interest in my
welfare, and that your insults spring from
friendship."

My soul saw very well that the part she
was playing on this occasion was no flattering one. She began, too, to perceive that the
warmth of the dispute had put the cause of
it out of sight. Profiting from this circumstance, she caused a further distraction by
saying to Joannetti, who at that moment
entered the room, "Make some coffee!"
The noise of the cups attracted all the
rebel's attention, who forthwith forgot
everything else. In like manner we show
children a toy to make them forget the un-
wholesome fruit for which they beg and
stamp.

While the water was being heated, I insensibly fell asleep. I enjoyed that delightful sensation about which I have
already entertained my readers, and which

you experience when you feel yourself to be dozing. The agreeable rattling Joannetti made with the coffee-pot reëchoed in my brain, and set all my sensitive nerves vibrating, just as a single harp-string when struck will make the octaves resound.

At last I saw as it were, a shadow pass before me. I opened my eyes, and there stood Joannetti. Ah, what an aroma! How agreeable a surprise! Coffee! Cream! A pyramid of dry toast! Good reader, come, breakfast with me!

XL.

Imagination.

WHAT. a wealth of delights has kind Nature given to those who can enjoy them. Who can count the innumerable phases they assume in different individuals, and at different periods of life! The confused remembrance of the pleasures of my boyhood sends a thrill through my heart. Shall I attempt to paint the joys of the youth whose soul glows with all the warmth of love, at an age when interest, ambition, hatred, and all the base passions that degrade and torment humanity are unknown to him, even by name?

During this age, too short, alas! the sun shines with a brightness it never displays in after-life; the air is then purer, the streams clearer and fresher, and nature has aspects, and the woods have paths, which in our riper age we never find again. O, what perfumes those flowers breathe! How delicious are those fruits! With what colors is the morning sky adorned! Men are all good, generous, kind-hearted; and women all lovely and faithful. On all sides we meet with cordiality, frankness, and unselfishness. Nature presents to us nothing but flowers, virtues, and pleasures.

The excitement of love, and the anticipation of happiness, do they not fill our hearts to the brim with emotions no less lively and various?

The sight of nature and its contemplation, whether we regard it as a whole, or examine its details, opens to our reason an immense field of enjoyments. Soon the imagination, brooding over this sea of pleasures, increases their number and intensity. The various sensations so unite and blend as to form new ones. Dreams of glory mingle with the palpitations of love. Benevolence moves hand in hand with self-esteem. Melancholy, from time to time, throws over us her solemn livery, and changes our tears to joy. Thus the perceptions of the mind, the feelings of the heart, the very remembrance of sensations, are inexhaustible sources of pleasure and comfort to man. No wonder, then, that the noise Joannetti made with the coffee-pot, and the unexpected appearance of a cup of cream, should have impressed me so vividly and so agreeably.

XLI.

The Travelling-coat.

I PUT on my travelling-coat, after having . examined it with a complacent eye ; and forthwith resolved to write a chapter *ad hoc*, that I might make it known to the reader. .

The form and usefulness of these garments being pretty generally known, I will treat specially of their influence upon the minds of travellers.

My winter travelling-coat is made of the warmest and softest stuff I could meet with. It envelops me entirely from head to foot, and when I am in my arm-chair, with my hands in my pockets, I am very like the statue of Vishnu one sees in the pagodas of India.

You may, if you will, tax me with prejudice when I assert the influence a traveller's costume exercises upon its wearer.
At any rate I can confidently affirm with
regard to this matter, that it would appear
to me as ridiculous to take a single step of
my journey round my room in uniform,
with my sword at my side, as it would to
go forth into the world in my dressing-
gown. Were I to find myself in full
military dress, not only should I be unable
to proceed with my journey, but I really
believe I should not be able to read what I
have written about my travels, still less to
understand it.

Does this surprise you? Do we not
every day meet with people who fancy
they are ill because they are unshaven, or
because some one has thought they have
looked poorly, and told them so? Dress
has such influence upon men's minds that
there are valetudinarians who think them-

selves in better health than usual when they have on a new coat and well-powdered wig. They deceive the public and themselves by their nicety about dress, until one finds some fine morning they have died in full fig, and their death startles everybody.

And in the class of men among whom I live, how many there are who, finding themselves clothed in uniform, firmly believe they are officers, until the unexpected appearance of the enemy shows them their mistake. And more than this, if it be the king's good pleasure to allow one of them to add to his coat a certain trimming, he straightway believes himself to be a general, and the whole army gives him the title without any notion of making fun of him! So great an influence has a coat upon the human imagination!

The following illustration will show still further the truth of my assertion.

It sometimes happened that they forgot to inform the Count de —— some days beforehand of the approach of his turn to mount guard. Early one morning, on the very day on which this duty fell to the Count, a corporal awoke him, and announced the disagreeable news. But the idea of getting up there and then, putting on his gaiters, and turning out without having thought about it the evening before, so disturbed him that he preferred reporting himself sick and staying at home all day. So he put on his dressing-gown, and sent away his barber. This made him look pale and ill, and frightened his wife and family. He really *did* feel a little poorly.

He told every one he was not very well, partly for the sake of appearances, and partly because he positively believed himself to be indisposed. Gradually the influence of the dressing-gown began to work.

The slops he was obliged to take upset his stomach. His relations and friends sent to ask after him. He was soon quite ill enough to take to his bed.

In the evening Dr. Ranson[1] found his pulse hard and feverish, and ordered him to be bled next day,

If the campaign had lasted a month longer, the sick man's case would have been past cure.

Now, who can doubt about the influence of travelling-coats upon travellers, if he reflect that poor Count de —— thought more than once that he was about to perform a journey to the other world for having inopportunely donned his dressing-gown in this?

[1] A popular Turin physician when the *Voyage* was written.

VÉTISSIER D.   GUILLAUME G.

XLII.

Aspasia's Buskin.

I WAS sitting near my fire after dinner, enveloped in my " habit de voyage," and freely abandoning myself to · its influence : the hour for starting was, I knew, drawing nigh ; but the fumes generated by digestion rose to my brain, and so obstructed the channels along which thoughts glide on their way from the senses, that all communication between them was intercepted. And as my senses no longer transmitted any idea to my brain, the latter, in its turn, could no longer emit any of that electric fluid with which the ingenious Doctor Valli resuscitates dead frogs.

After reading this preamble, you will easily understand why my head fell on my chest, and why the muscles of the thumb and forefinger of my right hand, being no longer excited by the electric fluid, became so relaxed that a volume of the works of the Marquis Caraccioli, which I was holding tightly between these two fingers, imperceptibly eluded my grasp, and fell upon the hearth.

I had just had some callers, and my conversation with the persons who had left the room had turned upon the death of Dr. Cigna, an eminent physician then lately deceased. He was a learned and hard-working man, a good naturalist, and a famous botanist. My thoughts were occupied with the merits of this skillful man. "And yet," I said to myself, "were it possible for me to evoke the spirits of those whom he has, perhaps, dismissed to the other world, who knows but that his reputation might suffer some diminution?"

I travelled insensibly to a dissertation on medicine and the progress it has made since the time of Hippocrates. I asked myself whether the famous personages of antiquity who died in their beds, as Pericles, Plato, the celebrated Aspasia, and Hippocrates, died, after the manner of ordinary mortals, of some putrid or inflammatory fever ; and whether they were bled, and crammed with specifics.

To say why these four personages came into my mind rather than any others, is out of my power ; for who can give reasons for what he dreams ? All that I can say is that my soul summoned the doctor of Cos, the doctor of Turin, and the famous statesman who did such great things, and committed such grave faults.

But as to his graceful friend, I humbly own that it was the OTHER who beckoned her to come. Still, however, when I think of the interview, I am tempted to feel some little pride, for it is evident that in this dream the balance in favor of reason was as four to one. Pretty fair this, methinks, for a lieutenant.

However this may be, whilst giving myself up to the reflections I have described, my eyes closed, and I fell fast asleep. But upon shutting my eyes, the image of the personages of whom I had been thinking, remained painted upon that delicate canvas we call memory; and these images, mingling in my brain with the idea of the evocation of the dead, it was not long before I saw advancing in procession Hippocrates, Plato, Pericles, Aspasia, and Doctor Cigna in his bob-wig.

I saw them all seat themselves in chairs ranged around the fire. Pericles alone remained standing to read the newspapers.

"If the discoveries of which you speak were true," said Hippocrates to the doctor, "and had they been as useful to the healing art as you affirm, I should have seen . the number of those who daily descend to the gloomy realm of Pluto decrease; but the ratio of its inhabitants, according to the registers of Minos which I have myself verified, remains still the same as formerly."

Doctor Cigna turned to me and said: "You have without doubt heard these discoveries spoken of. You know that Harvey discovered the circulation of the blood; that the immortal Spallanzani explained the process of digestion, the mechanism of which is now well understood;" and he entered upon a long detail of all the discoveries connected with physic, and of the host of remedies for which we are indebted to chemistry: in short, he delivered an academical discourse in favor of modern medicine.

" But am I to believe," I replied, " that these great men were ignorant of all you have been telling them, and that their souls, having shuffled off this mortal coil, still meet with any obscurities in nature ? "

" Ah ! how great is your error ! " exclaimed the *proto-physician*[1] of the Peloponnesus. The mysteries of nature are as closely hidden from the dead as from the living. Of one thing we who linger on the banks of the Styx are certain, that He who created all things alone knows the great secret which men vainly strive to solve. And," added he, turning to the doctor, " do be persuaded by me to divest yourself of what still clings to you of the party-spirit you have brought with you from the sojourn of mortals. And since, seeing that Charon daily ferries over in his boat as many shades as heretofore, the labors of a thousand generations and all the discov-

---

[1] A title known at the Sardinian court.

eries men have made have not been able to prolong their existence, let us not uselessly weary ourselves in defending an art which, among the dead, cannot even profit its practitioners."

Thus, to my great amazement, spoke the famous Hippocrates.

Doctor Cigna smiled ; and as spirits can neither withstand evidence, nor silence truth, he not only agreed with Hippocrates, but, blushing after the manner of disembodied intelligences, he protested that he had himself always had his doubts.

Pericles, who had drawn near the window, heaved a deep sigh, the cause of which I divined. He was reading a number of the "Moniteur," which announced the decadence of the arts and sciences. He saw illustrious scholars desert their sublime conceptions to invent new crimes, and shuddered at hearing a rabble herd compare themselves with the heroes of

generous Greece ; and this, forsooth, because they put to death, without shame or
remorse, venerable old men, women, and
children, and coolly perpetrated the black-
est and most useless crimes.

Plato, who had listened to our conversation without joining in it, and seeing it
brought to a sudden and unexpected close,
thus spoke: " I can readily understand
that the discoveries great men have made
in the various branches of natural science
do not forward the art of medicine, which
can never change the course of nature,
except at the cost of life. But this will
certainly not be so with the researches
that have been made in the study of
politics. Locke's inquiries into the nature
of the human understanding, the invention
of printing, the accumulated observations
drawn from history, the number of excellent books which have spread sound infor-
mation even among the lower orders, — so

many wonders must have contributed to make men better, and the happy republic I , conceived, which the age in which I lived caused me to regard as an impracticable dream, no doubt now exists upon the earth?" At this question the honest doctor cast down his eyes, and only answered by tears. In wiping them with his pocket-handkerchief, he involuntarily moved his wig on one side, so that a part of his face was hidden by it. "Ye gods!" exclaimed Aspasia, with a scream, "how strange a sight! And is it a discovery of one of your great men that has led you to the idea of turning another man's skull into a head-dress?"

Aspasia, from whom our philosophical dissertations had elicited nothing but gapes, had taken up a magazine of fashions which lay on the chimney-piece, the leaves of which she had been turning over for some time when the doctor's wig made

10

her utter this exclamation. Finding the
, narrow, ricketty seat upon which, she was
sitting uncomfortable, she had, without the
least ceremony, placed her two bare legs,
which were adorned with bandelets, on the
straw-bottomed chair between her and me,
and rested her elbow upon the broad
shoulders of Plato.

"It is no skull," said the doctor, addressing her, and taking off his wig, which
he threw on the fire, "it is a wig, madam ;
and I know not why I did not cast this
ridiculous ornament into the flames of
Tartarus when first I came among you.
But absurdities and prejudices adhere so
closely to our miserable nature that they
even follow us sometimes beyond the
grave." I took singular pleasure in seeing
the doctor thus abjure his physic and his
wig at the same moment.

"I assure you," said Aspasia, "that most
of the head-dresses represented in the

pages I have been turning over deserve the same fate as yours, so very extravagant are they."

The fair Athenian amused herself vastly in looking over the engravings, and was very reasonably surprised by the variety and oddity of modern contrivances. One figure, especially struck her. It was that of a young lady with a really elegant head-dress which Aspasia only thought some-what too high. But the piece of gauze that covered the neck was so very full you could scarcely see half her face. Aspasia, not knowing that these extraordinary developments were produced by starch, could not help showing a surprise which would have been redoubled (but inversely), had the gauze been transparent.

" But do explain," she said, " why women of the present day seem to wear dresses to hide rather than to clothe them. They scarcely allow their faces to be seen, those faces by which alone their sex is to be guessed, so strangely are their bodies disfigured by the eccentric folds of their garments. Among all the figures represented in these pages, I do not find one with the neck, arms, and legs bare. How is it your young warriors are not tempted to put an end to such a fashion? It would appear," she added, "that the virtue of the women of this age, which they parade in all their articles of dress, greatly surpasses that of my contemporaries."

As she ended these words, Aspasia turned her eyes on me as if to ask a reply. I pretended not to notice this, and in order to give myself an absent air, took up the tongs and pushed away among the embers the shreds of the doctor's wig which had escaped the flames. Observing presently afterwards that one of the bandelets which clasped Aspasia's buskin had come undone,

" Permit me," said I, " charming lady," —
and eagerly stooping, stretched out my
hands towards the chair on which I had
fancied I saw those legs about which even
great philosophers went into ecstacies.

I am persuaded that at this moment I
was very near genuine somnambulism, so
real was the movement of which I speak.
But Rose, who happened to be sleeping in
the chair, thought the movement was
meant for her, and jumping nimbly into
my arms, she drove back into Hades the
famous shades my travelling-coat had
summoned.

DELIGHTFUL realm of Imagination, which the benevolent Being has bestowed upon man to console him for the disappointments he meets with in real life.

This day, certain persons on whom I am dependent affect to restore me to liberty. As if they had ever deprived me of it! As if it were in their power to snatch it from me for a single moment, and to hinder me from traversing, at my own good pleasure, the vast space that ever lies open before me! They have forbidden me to go at large in a city, a mere speck, and have left open to me the whole universe, in which immensity and eternity obey me.

I am now free, then; or rather, I must enter again into bondage. The yoke of

office is again to weigh me down, and
every step I take must conform with the
exigencies of politeness and duty. Fortunate shall I be if some capricious goddess
do not again make me forget both, and if I
escape from this new and dangerous captivity.

O why did they not allow me to finish
my captivity! Was it as a punishment
that I was exiled to my chamber, to that
delightful country in which abound all the
riches and enjoyments of the world? As
well might they consign a mouse to a
granary.

Still, never did I more clearly perceive
that I am double than I do now. Whilst
I regret my imaginary joys, I feel myself
consoled. I am borne along by an unseen
power which tells me I need the pure air,
and the light of heaven, and that solitude is
like death. Once more I don my custom-
ary garb; my door opens; I wander under

the spacious porticos of the Strada della Po ; a thousand agreeable visions float before my eyes. Yes, there is that mansion, that door, that staircase ! I thrill with expectation.

In like manner the act of slicing a lemon gives you a foretaste that makes your mouth water.

Poor ANIMAL ! Take care !